The Movies

Chris Oxlade

First published in Great Britain by Heinemann Library
Halley Court, Jordan Hill, Oxford OX2 8EJ
a division of Reed Educational and Professional Publishing Ltd

OXFORD FLORENCE PRAGUE MADRID ATHENS
MELBOURNE AUCKLAND KUALA LUMPUR SINGAPORE TOKYO
IBADAN NAIROBI KAMPALA JOHANNESBURG GABORONE
PORTSMOUTH NH CHICAGO MEXICO CITY SAO PAULO

Designed by **AMR**
Illustrations by Art Construction
Originated in the UK by Dot Gradations Ltd, Wickford
Printed in the UK by Jarrold Printing Ltd, Thetford

00 99 98 97 96
10 9 8 7 6 5 4 3 2 1

ISBN 0 431 06448 2

British Library Cataloguing in Publication Data
Oxlade, Chris
Movies. – (Making science work)
1. Motion pictures – Juvenile literature
I. Title
791.4'3'01

Acknowledgements
The publishers would like to thank the following for permission to reproduce
photographs. The Ronald Grant Archive: p.4 (bottom), p.12 (bottom), p.24, p.26; BFI
Stills, Posters and Designs: p.5, p.10, p.17, p.18, p.20, p.22; Michael Holford: p.6, p.7 (top);
The Science Museum/Science and Society Picture Library: p.7 (bottom); Nick Yates: p.8,
p.14, p.21; The Kobal Collection: p.12 (top), p.16, p.28, p.29; National Museum of
Photography, Film and Television: p.25; JNTO: p.27.

Cover photograph reproduced with the permission of The Ronald Grant Archive.

Our thanks to Jim Drake for his comments in the preparation of this book.
Every effort has been made to contact copyright holders of any material reproduced in
this book. Any omissions will be rectified in subsequent printings if notice is given to the
Publisher.

CONTENTS

INTRODUCTION

As you sit in your comfortable cinema seat, eating popcorn and watching the latest blockbusting movie, you probably don't think about how the movie was actually made. In this book, you can find out how science is used on a movie **set**, when the movie is edited and when it is shown in the cinema. You can also find out how science and technology make amazing special effects possible.

Recording pictures and sound

The word 'movie' is short for moving picture. It is called a moving picture because the people and things you see in it appear to move as they do in real life. A cine-camera is used to film the pictures for a movie. The images are recorded on a very long strip of plastic film. A cine-camera takes photographs in the same way as an ordinary stills camera – but it takes them very quickly, one after another, and spaces them along the film. The actors' voices are recorded on **magnetic tape**. The pictures and sounds are recorded in small chunks called **takes**. There will be a piece of film for each take.

Inside a modern cinema. The screen is behind a fireproof curtain.

Movie sets look chaotic, but each person is doing a particular job.

utting it together

film editor puts together the final film. The
itor starts with all the pieces of film and the
und tapes. He or she selects the good bits of
n, throws some bits away and joins everything
gether. The sound and any special effects are
o added to the film.

the cinema

e film arrives at the cinema in two or three
ng rolls called **reels**. A projector shines light
rough the film which enables you to see the
cture on the cinema screen. The projector also
produces the film's sound.

ry to imagine the months of work that
have gone into the next action movie you
ee.

INVENTIONS GALORE!

Thomas Alva Edison
(1847–1931) was a
famous American
inventor. He invented
the first sound recording
machine and the
microphone, and built
the first electric power
station. He also invented
the kinetoscope, which
showed motion pictures.
Only one person at a
time could view the
pictures through a small
eyepiece.

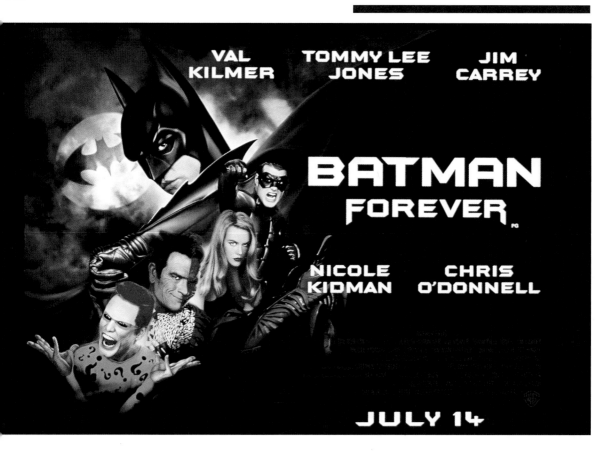

MAKING MOVIES MOVE

Look at something in the room and then close your eyes tightly very quickly. You will find that your eyes 'remember' what you were looking at for a split second before everything goes dark. This effect is called **persistence of vision**, and movies depend on it. A movie is made up of thousands of pictures, each one slightly different from the one before. Each picture is called a **frame**. When you watch the movie, you see the frames one after the other in quick succession. In fact, you see 24 frames every second. Persistence of vision means that you do not see the gaps between the frames, and you are fooled into thinking you are seeing a moving picture.

THOUSANDS OF FRAMES

A movie is filmed and shown at the rate of 24 frames every second. A movie that lasts for an hour and a half (90 minutes) contains $90 \times 60 \times 24 = 129{,}600$ frames! The actual film is over 1.8 miles (3 kilometres) long.

Moving picture toys

In the middle of the nineteenth century, before movies were ever thought of, toys which produced moving pictures were very popular with children (and adults!). The toys made use of persistence of vision, just as modern movies do. The simplest toy was called a thaumatrope. It was a disc with a picture on each side. When you spun the disc, the two pictures appeared quickly, one after the other, and combined into one picture. Other toys, such as the zoetrope and phenakistiscope, showed moving pictures made up of ten or more frames. All the pictures were drawn by hand because there were no cine-cameras to film real objects as they moved.

This is a zoetrope. When you spin the cylinder and look through the slots, you see a moving picture.

irst photos

otography started early in
e nineteenth century. At
at time, scientists realized
at certain chemicals
ange into other
emicals when light
ines on them. Early
otographs were taken
er a period of several
nutes because the
emicals changed only very
owly.
otographic
emicals
ere
adually
proved, and by
e 1870s
otographs could be
ken in a fraction of a
cond. By this time,
otographers could take
otographs in quick succession to record moving
ings. In the 1890s a French scientist, Etienne
les Marey, built a movie camera and projector.
e used them to record and show the movement of
imals and people in **slow motion**.

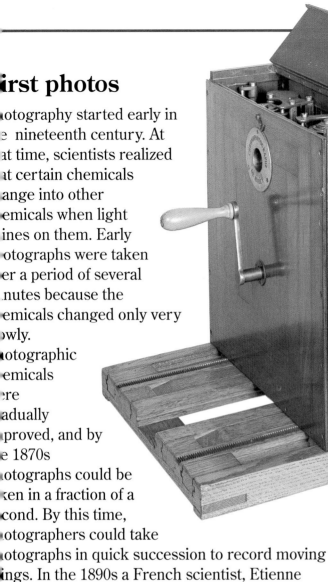

Marey's movie camera
and projector of the
1890s was able to record
and show slow motion
movement.

This piece of Marey's
work shows a man
jumping, in slow motion.
You can see each move
made in the jump.

FILMING A MOVIE

ave you ever wondered how film records action? Moving pictures are photographed by cine-cameras. The camera's job is to take a photograph, wind on the film inside the camera, take another photograph, move the film on again, and so on. The **lens** at the front of the camera collects light from the scene being photographed and shines it on to the film. The film contains chemicals which change into different chemicals when light hits them. Where more light reaches the film, the chemicals change more. In this way, the film records the scene.

Getting in focus

We see an object because our eyes detect some of the light rays that are reflected from it. At the front of each eye there is a lens. It collects light rays from a scene and shines them onto the light-sensitive retina at the back of each eye. A cine-camera works in the same way. Its lens bends the rays so that all the rays coming from one place in the scene hit the same place on the film. This makes a sharp, focused image on the film. If the rays do not hit the same place on the film, the image is blurred. The camera's shutter opens to let light hit the film, and then closes while the film is moved on.

The large drums on a cine-camera contain hundreds of metres of film

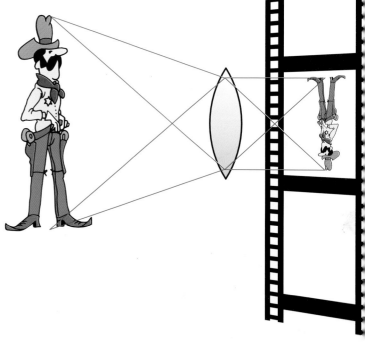

Two rays from each point in the scene are focused on to the film.

oom in and out

ost cine-cameras have a om lens. It allows the film-aker to get a close-up view of tors' faces, for example, or show a wide panorama.

zoom lens can work like a lescope so that just a small rt of the scene appears, agnified, in the image. This called telephoto. The lens n also make a very large ea of the scene appear, duced, in the image. This is lled wide angle.

UNDERWATER CAMERAS

As a diver goes deeper underwater, the water presses on the diver's body more and more. The same **pressure** acts on underwater cameras. They have strong metal cases, with rubber seals to withstand the pressure, so that water does not leak into the camera. Underwater cameras are painted yellow to make them visible in the gloomy deep-sea light.

Top: the normal view of a scene.
Middle: the view with the zoom set to telephoto.
Bottom: the view with the zoom set to wide angle.

SOUNDTRACKS

As you watch a movie, you hear the soundtrack at the same time. The soundtrack is normally contained on a narrow strip of magnetic material down the side of the film, next to the **frames** of pictures. It is rather like having the tape from a cassette glued along the film. The soundtrack is recorded onto the film by making magnetic patterns in the strip. When the film is shown, the sound is reproduced by loudspeakers in the cinema. How is sound recorded?

Recording sound

When something makes a noise, it makes the air around it vibrate. The vibrations spread out quickly. You can hear the sound when the vibrations reach your ears. On a film **set**, the actors' voices are detected by microphones. These turn the sounds into **electrical signals**, which are recorded on a **magnetic tape**. Sometimes voices are recorded after filming has been completed in a process called **dubbing**. The movie's music and sound effects are recorded on other tapes. All the sounds are then mixed together by a sound engineer to make the final soundtrack.

To collect sounds, the sound technician holds the microphone near the actors. It is supported on a long pole called a boom.

ound on film

movie's soundtrack is sometimes recorded on
e film as a pattern of light and dark. Inside the
ojector, a light is shone through the film. A light
tector on the other side detects the changing
ght pattern and turns it into an electrical signal.
ne signal is sent to the loudspeakers which
ange it back into the sounds we hear.

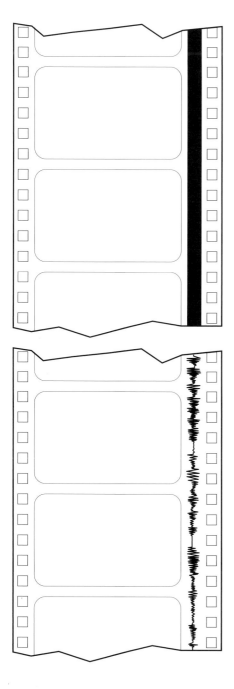

IN TIME

The pictures and
sounds on the final film
must be exactly in time
with each other. The
process of making sure
that this happens is
called synchronization.
A clapper board is
snapped shut in front
of the camera at the
start of each **take**. The
point on the picture
frame where it closes
can be matched with
the soundtrack because
of the snapping noise
that it makes.

Top: a magnetic soundtrack
on a 35-mm film.
Bottom: an optical soundtrack
on a similar film.

BRIGHT LIGHTS

Movie **sets** and film studios always have plenty of bright lights. Why are these bright lights, called lamps, needed? It is mainly because lighting makes the scene bright enough for the film in the cine-camera to record it. The lamps do the same job as a flash gun on a normal camera. Lighting is especially important in a studio or on a dull day outdoors. Film-makers also use lighting to create dramatic scenes. Spot lamps can light up just one area of a scene, and coloured lamps make actors and sets look weird or spooky.

Making a beam of light

Every lamp has a bulb. Inside the bulb is a thin coil of wire called a filament. When electricity flows through the filament, the filament gets so hot that it glows very brightly. Light spreads out in all directions from the bulb. A mirror behind the bulb reflects any light going backwards, and sends it out of the front of the lamp. Spot lamps also have a lens at the front to concentrate the light into a narrow beam.

Low-angle spot lighting casts a tall, spooky shadow of the actress and stair rail.

Here, lighting comes from the sun and spot lamps. Extra light can be cast on the scene by large, flat, white sheets called reflectors.

olours and filters

nlight is made from a mixture of many different
lours of light. It is called white light. You can see
e different colours of light in a rainbow. The light
lbs that you use at home give out light which is
ite yellow. If this kind of bulb were used to light a
ovie set, the final picture would look too yellow.
ovie lamps, like other photographic lamps,
oduce natural-looking white light. Coloured light
made by sliding a **filter** over the lamp. The filter
ops light rays of all the colours except for the
lour needed, which it lets pass through.

A spot of coloured light
produced by a spot lamp and
coloured filter.

The power of a light is
measured in the
number of watts of
electricity that it uses.
A torch bulb has a
power of about 1 watt
(1 W). Domestic light
bulbs have a power of
between 40 and 100
watts. A movie-set
lamp has a power of
several thousand watts.

FROM CAMERA TO CINEMA

What happens to a film after it has been used in a cine-camera? The chemicals on the film contain the images of each **frame** of the moving picture. They are not images that you can see, but simply patterns of different chemicals in the film. The film must be kept in complete darkness. If any light gets onto it, the chemicals will change again and the images will be spoiled. The film is taken to a processing laboratory. Here, it goes through a chemical process which turns the chemical images into real pictures that you can see.

Colour films

All the colours of the rainbow can be made up by mixing red, blue and green light together, in different amounts. A colour film has three layers: one is sensitive to blue light, one to red light and one to green light. Yellow light, for example, is a mixture of red and green light. When the camera films a yellow object, the red and green layers of the film react, but the blue layer does not. When this film is developed, the red layer turns red and the green layer turns green where the light has hit the film. When light shines through the developed film, the coloured layers act as **filters** and turn the light into the right colour.

A commercial cine-film processing laboratory. The film moves gradually through tanks of chemicals.

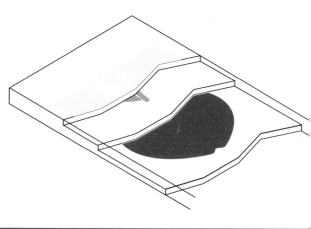

A cut-away of a developed colour film. The layers are supported by plastic.

A film editor at work in the film-editing suite. The editing machine allows quick and accurate cutting and splicing.

ilm editing

movie is not filmed in one continuous **take**.
kes can be a few seconds or a few minutes long,
d there may be several takes for the same scene.
hen the film is processed, a film editor selects the
st pieces and joins them together to make the
al film. This is done by cutting between the
mes and joining, or splicing, them together with
e. Finally, the film is copied on to one or two
g pieces of film. It is then copied again lots of
es and sent out to be shown in cinemas.

LOST FILMS

Early movies were photographed on film that gradually deteriorated as the chemicals on it reacted with the air. Many movies have been lost because the film has been destroyed this way. Later movies have since been photographed on film that does not deteriorate.

SPECIAL EFFECTS

H ow did the toys in *Toy Story* come to life? How did the dinosaurs in *Jurassic Park* run? The answer is by special effects. Special effects are produced by photographic tricks and computer graphics.

Flying on film

Special effects experts have had several different ways of making actors in a studio look as though they are somewhere completely different. To show a person flying through the air, for example, the actor is filmed in a flying position in a studio. The background is shot on another piece of film. The two films are then mixed photographically to make the actor appear to be flying across the background. A 'hole' is created in the background, which is then filled by the 'flying' actor. Today, computers are used instead. First, the different pieces of film are scanned and stored in the computer. The scanning process divides the picture into millions of tiny coloured squares. Any bits of film from one take can be cut out and added to another take. Finally, a special printer turns the computer images back into real film.

Special effects allow Superman and Lois Lane t[o] fly above the Earth.

Actors are normally filmed against a plain background to make it easier to cut their images out of the background and add them on to another one.

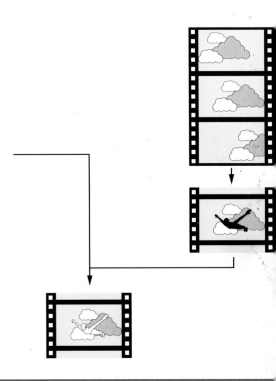

omputer effects

mputers can produce very convincing pictures of
d or imaginary creatures and scenes. These can
o be mixed with real **footage**. Film-makers use
mputer graphics to create amazing special
ects. People can use computers to draw pictures
anything – and it doesn't have to be a drawing of
hing that exists in the real world. Once a model
say, a dinosaur, has been created inside the
mputer, the dinosaur can be viewed from any
gle, and with any sort of lighting. If the dinosaur
eated by computer graphics is to be mixed with
ıl film, the real lighting and the lighting of the
mputer image must be carefully matched.

Roger Rabbit was created by computer and
nixed into the real footage. Of course the
ıctor, Bob Hoskins, had to imagine Roger
vas there.

The American Stephen
Spielberg (born 1946) is
one of the most
successful modern movie
producers. His movies
include *Jaws*, *E.T.* and
Jurassic Park. Most of his
movies contain amazing
special effects.

STUNT ACTION

Although many special effects are created with camera tricks or computer graphics, others are produced with models and **slow-motion** filming. Some dangerous pieces of action still have to be performed by specially trained people. They are known as stunt people. When they are driving in car chases, jumping from windows or running through fires, stunt people need to work with great accuracy and split-second timing.

Stunts

Stunt people have to understand how things fall, fly, burn, skid and so on so that their stunts look realistic. At the same time the stunts need to be as safe as possible to perform. For a simple stunt, such as a fall from a roof, the stunt person lands on a soft mattress. The greater the drop, the faster the stunt person is travelling when he or she reaches the ground, and so the deeper the cushion needs to be. When stunts involve cars flying off cliffs or turning over on ramps, careful calculations are made to work out where the car will land.

Filming a scene fro the movie *Backdra* Stage hands are close by with fire extinguishers.

Fire safety

Many action films involve fires and explosions. Sometimes stunt people have to go into a fire or be set alight. They wear fire-resistant clothing which helps to protect them until the **take** is finished. The flames are put out immediately after the take with fire extinguishers. To create an explosion, the amount of explosive used is carefully calculated so that it produces a good effect without endangering the actors or film crew.

Models like this hand have to be made and filmed very carefully, and as realistically as possible, so that they look lifelike and scary.

Modelling stunts

...m-makers use models of things such as sinking ...ips or crashing aircraft for some action ...quences. Special filming techniques are needed, ...wever, to make them look convincing. Special ...ects technicians understand that all objects fall ...wnwards at the same rate when they are ...opped. For example, a real helicopter would fall ...the same way as a much smaller model one. But ...he model is filmed normally, it will appear to fall ...naturally fast, so it is photographed with the film ...nning more quickly than normal. When the film ...viewed at normal speed, the action looks natural.

A TRUE STORY?

In the movie *True Lies*, an actor jumps from a skyscraper on to the top of a Harrier jet hovering outside the building. In reality, the actor, aircraft and skyscraper were all filmed separately. The films were put together on a computer to create the scene you see in the movie.

ANIMATED MOVIES

How do film-makers create cartoons? How do they bring puppets and models to life? The answer is by animation, the process of making inanimate (non-living) objects appear to move. Animated films are made by photographing cartoon pictures or

models one by one. Each photograph makes up one **frame** of the film. After each frame, the cartoon pictures or models are moved a small amount, then another frame is photographed, and so on. This method of filming is called stop-frame photography. When the final film is viewed at the correct speed, you are tricked into thinking you are seeing a moving picture.

The Wallace and Gromit film are created by stop-frame photography of the models.

Drawing cartoons

To make a cartoon, a separate picture is drawn for each frame. Each frame is slightly different from the previous one. The characters and backgrounds are drawn separately on transparent plastic sheets called cells. This means that the background does not have to be drawn again and again. The background can be split into different parts and moved slightly along in each frame to give the impression of movement.

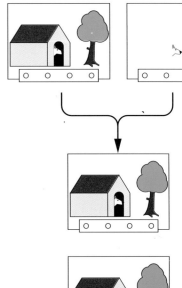
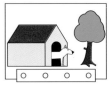
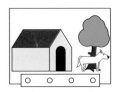

Animation cells. The kennel is drawn just once, but a bit more of the dog is visible in each frame.

computer cartoons

...day, many cartoons are drawn by computer. ...tists sketch the shapes of the film's characters, ...ich are then copied into the computer and ...loured. The artist draws a picture for every few ...mes, and the the computer works out what the ...mes in between need to look like to make the ...aracter's movements smooth. When the cartoon ...complete, the frames are transferred from the ...mputer on to film.

Models and puppets

...odels and puppets can be animated by ...otographing them in one position, moving them ...ghtly, photographing them again, and so on. ...hen working with models of animals or people, ...imators must understand how they move in real ...e in order to make them look convincing to us ...en we see the film. Model animation is filmed by ...ing a camera to a **dolly** or tripod in a studio. The ...mera can be moved and zoomed for each step.

The pink figure is being animated. The camera is specially adapted to take stop-frame films.

SHOWING A MOVIE

Have you ever wondered how movies are shown at the cinema? At the back of the cinema is a projector. It shines light through the film and onto the cinema screen, making a huge copy of the image on the film. Light hits the screen and bounces off into your eyes so you can see the image. The projector shows each **frame** of the film for just a fraction of a second before moving the film onto the next frame for a fraction of a second, and so on.

The projector

The projector has a very powerful bulb which makes an extremely bright white light. This light is needed to produce a picture on the screen which is bright enough for you to see. A **lens** collects the light rays from the bulb and shines them onto the back of the film. When the light passes through the film, it becomes coloured. The projector lens focuses the light rays onto the screen. It makes sure that light rays from the same point on the film strike the same point on the screen.

Inside the projection room of a cinema. The pictures are projected through the window in the front wall.

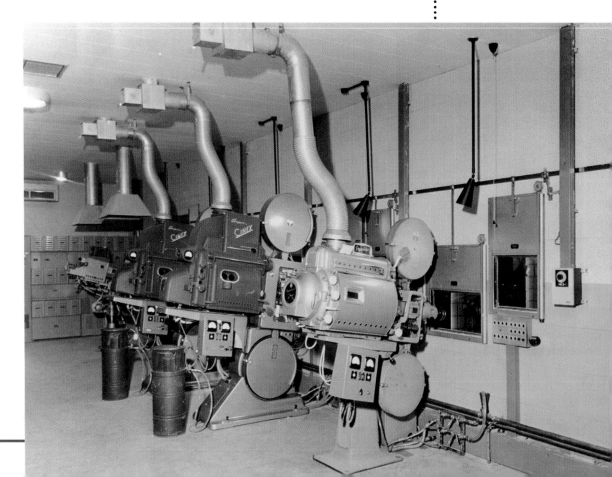

On screen

The cinema screen reflects light rays from the projector back into the eyes of the audience. It scatters the rays so that you see them coming from all parts of the screen, wherever you are sitting in the cinema. Close up, the screen is quite rough, like a sheet of rough paper. If the screen was very smooth, light rays hitting one part of the screen would bounce off towards some people in the cinema and not others.

Hear the sound

The film's soundtrack is picked up by the projector, which turns it into an **electrical signal**. The signal is sent to loudspeakers. The speakers turn the electrical signal into vibrating sound waves that you can hear. The speakers are normally placed behind the screen, which has thousands of tiny holes in its surface. The sound vibrations travel through these holes. In larger cinemas, the **acoustics** of the building make sure that no **echoes** are reflected from large flat areas such as the walls or ceiling. The ceiling is often covered in objects specially shaped to scatter the sound.

KEEPING COOL

Bright lights make a lot of heat. The heat from a projector lamp can make the film buckle (crumple) because the darker parts of the film become hot and expand. Cool air is blown across the film to prevent this from happening.

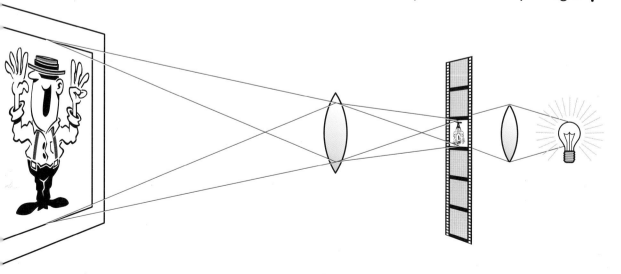

A projector creating an image on a cinema screen. The lens can move backwards and forwards to produce a sharp image.

BIG PICTURES

Movie pictures are not all the same size and shape. The pictures that you watch on the cinema screen are rectangular, and usually measure about 10 metres wide and about 7 metres high. In the 1950s and 1960s, wide-screen movies were popular. Wide screens give the audience a much better feeling of being on the actual movie **set**. Recently, movie-makers have used screens that are so big that they fill your whole **field of vision**. This means that you cannot see the sides of the screen, and your brain is fooled into thinking that you are really in the scene. Some screens are 30 metres high and wide, and cover one whole wall of the cinema.

Film formats

The width of a roll of film, and the way in which the frames and soundtrack fit onto it, are called the film **format**. Most movies are photographed on 35-mm film (which is 35 mm wide). Wide-screen and IMAX formats are photographed on film that is 70 mm wide.

Wide-screen movies

Cinerama and CinemaScope were two kinds of wide-screen movie invented in the 1950s. Cinerama worked by projecting three films next to each other on a huge curved screen. Three cameras were used to film each scene of the movie. A CinemaScope camera had a special **lens** which squashed a picture of a wide scene into a normal-sized frame. The projector's lens reversed the process. Many wide-screen movies were made in the 1950s and 1960s, but this format became less popular in the 1970s.

The Cinerama wide-screen system was perfect for showing the natural world and action rides.

MAX movies

Modern large-screen movies are photographed on large-format film to produce an enormous and very clear picture. They are known as IMAX (Image Maximum) movies. If a normal film is shown at this size, it looks dim and blurred because not enough detail has been recorded on the film itself. Because the picture on the large screen is so huge, a tiny vibration in the projector can make the picture shake. To avoid this problem, IMAX projectors are very heavy. Also, they are mounted on rubber feet to help stop vibrations.

Inside an IMAX cinema, the screen is as tall as seven elephants standing on top of each other!

CINEMA IN THE ROUND

In 1955, Walt Disney built a circular cinema which gave an all-round, 360-degree view. It took eleven projectors to show the pictures. The viewers stood in the middle of the circle.

MORE MOVIE TRICKS

Showing films on huge screens is one way of making a movie seem realistic. What other tricks do movie-makers use to make movies seem real?

3-D films

The images in a 3-D film look like real, solid objects, rather than just flat pictures. As your eyes are set a few centimetres apart, each eye sees a slightly different view of a scene. This allows you to see things in three **dimensions**, and to judge how far away objects are. Photographs and movies look flat because each eye sees the same picture. Three-dimensional films are photographed by two cameras side by side. One photographs the view your right eye would see, while the other photographs the view your left eye would see. In the cinema, two projectors project the film onto the same screen. The projectors are fitted with special coloured **filters**, and the audience wears glasses with filters of the same colour. One eye sees light from one projector and the other eye sees light from the other projector. Your brain is fooled into seeing the scenes in three dimensions.

This audience is watching a 3-D movie through special glasses.

The screens these theme-park riders are watching are inside their helmets. This is called virtual reality. Motion-control seats make it more realistic.

Simulator rides

Many theme parks have simulator rides. On the ride, you sit in a seat and watch movie pictures which completely fill your **field of vision**. As you watch the movie you feel as if you are hurtling through a landscape. The seat moves under you at the same time. The movie and seat movements are carefully synchronized. This fools your senses of touch and balance as well as your sight. The effect can be frighteningly realistic! Some cinemas have been built with motion-control seats.

HOW MANY FRAMES?

A team of American movie-makers has carried out experiments to see how viewers' brains react to movies filmed at different **frame rates**. They found that a rate of 60 frames a second (instead of the normal 24) gives the most realistic effect.

MOVIES ABOUT SCIENCE

You have already seen how science plays its part in making and showing movies. But how do scientific things themselves appear in the movies? Movie-makers try to make the science in their films as convincing as possible. They ask scientists from many different subject areas – physicists, biologists, medical experts and so on – to advise them when they are writing scripts and building movie **sets** and **props**.

Fact or fiction?

Unfortunately, knowledge about science facts sometimes makes it difficult to make a good, exciting movie! Sometimes they have to be ignored as, for example, in movies about such fantastic subjects as the monster created by Dr Frankenstein; the monster is built from parts of dead people and brought to life with electricity! Or the audience has to believe that the characters in the movie have developed new scientific techniques or new technologies. Real scientists do not believe that dinosaurs can be brought back to life as they were in *Jurassic Park*. And in the movies, computers always seem to be much more clever than in real life!

New scientific techniques make dinosaurs come back to life in *Jurassic Park*.

Journey to the Moon was made in 1902, 67 years before the first astronaut walked on the Moon. In the film, a professor is launched to the Moon in a large bullet fired from a cannon.

Fiction becomes fact

Science-fiction films are about aliens, future worlds and time travel. Movie-makers invent new scientific ideas and technologies to include in their science-fiction films. They make their fictional ideas convincing to us by basing them on actual scientific ideas. Some of the earliest films were science-fiction movies. The ideas in them, such as people going to the Moon, must have seemed ridiculous when the movies were first made. Yet many have already come true. Perhaps we shall bring a tyrannosaurus back to life one day!

SPACE RUBBISH

In the 1995 film *Apollo 13*, the damaged Apollo spacecraft drifts through space, leaving behind a trail of debris from an explosion on board. In reality, this could never happen – the debris would drift along with the spacecraft!

GLOSSARY

acoustics the study of sound. The acoustics of a room describe the way in which sound travels around it.

dimension the size of an object in one direction or another. A movie screen has two dimensions – length and width. A three-dimensional movie has depth from front to back as well.

dubbing the process of adding voices to a movie after the original pictures have been shot without recording the voices. The actors watch themselves on the film and speak the lines to match.

echo a reflected sound. Echoes happen when sound vibrations reach a solid surface and bounce back off it.

dolly a platform on wheels for a television or motion-picture camera

electrical signal an electric current which changes its strength and direction. In sound-recording equipment, the changes represent the vibrations of the sound.

field of vision the whole area of a scene that you can see at one time without moving your eyes up or down, or from side to side

filter a piece of glass or plastic which changes any light shining through it. Colour filters stop some colours of light and let other colours pass through.

footage a piece of film. The word 'footage' comes from 'foot', which is used to measure the length of a piece of film.

format the size of a film, and the way in which the frames and soundtrack are organized on it

frame a single photograph in a sequence on a film

frame rate the number of frames of a film which are shown in each second. Most films are shown at a rate of 24 frames a second.

immersed to be surrounded by something. Large-screen movies and moving seats can immerse you in another world.

lens a piece of glass or clear plastic which bends light rays as they pass through it. All optical instruments, such as cameras, telescopes and microscopes, use lenses.

magnetic tape a ribbon of thin plastic. It is coated with material which can be magnetize. Sound and other information can be recorded on the tape by making a magnetic pattern.

persistence of vision the way that your eye 'remember' a scene for a split second, even when they can no longer see the scene. Movies appear to move because of persistenc of vision.

pressure the amount of force (a force is a push or a pull) which presses on a certain area. As you go down in water, the water pressure pushing down on you increases because of the weight of the water above you

props objects, such as furniture and vehicle which are put in a film set to make it look lik a real-life scene

reel a long piece of film which is rolled up tightly. Films are stored in reels inside lightproof containers.

set an area where actors perform in front of cameras. A set can be a real one, either indoors or outdoors, or built in a studio.

slow motion the slowed-down movement of a film. The effect is made by filming the actio at a certain frame-rate, and then projecting it a slower frame-rate.

take a short piece of action which is filmed. Film-makers film several takes of the same scene, and then choose the best take during editing.

FACT FILE

The first successful talking movie, or 'talkie' was *The Jazz Singer*, made in 1927. Before then, lines of speech appeared on the screen for the viewers to read, and a musician in the cinema played live music.

Korea has the largest cinema screen in the world. It is 33 metres wide and 28 metres high.

The first public film show was presented in Paris, France, in 1895, by Louis and Auguste Lumière. The short films were about everyday life in Paris.

Movies were originally thought of as just an interesting amusement. Louis Lumière said: 'Cinema is a technology without a future'.

The longest movie ever made lasted 48 hours. It was called *The Longest Most Meaningless Movie in the World.*

The Radio City Music Hall, in New York, USA, is the world's largest cinema. It has 5,874 seats.

INDEX